Poems from
Cardiff

Selected by Amy Wack

Seren is the book imprint of
Poetry Wales Press Ltd.
57 Nolton Street, Bridgend, Wales, CF31 3AE

www.serenbooks.com
facebook.com/SerenBooks
twitter@SerenBooks

Poems © Individual Authors
Selection © Amy Wack, 2019

ISBN: 978-1-78172-485-9

A CIP record for this title is available from the British Library.

The publisher acknowledges the financial assistance of the Welsh Books Council.

Cover photograph: © Lois Gobe / Cardiff Bay – Pierhead Building –
Wales Millennium Centre

Printed in the Czech Republic by Akcent Media Ltd.

Contents

Acknowledgements

We gratefully acknowledge the permission of the publishers of the titles from which these poems are taken:

Gillian Clarke: 'City' and 'Wing' from *A Recipe for Water* (Carcanet, 2009); **Oliver Reynolds**: 'Taff' is from a broadsheet 'Rhondda Tennpenn'orth'; **Gwyneth Lewis**: 'V' (from 'Welsh Espionage') is from *Chaotic Angels: Poems in English* (Bloodaxe, 2005); **Damian Walford Davies**: 'Bestiary' from *Docklands* (Seren, 2019); **Mab Jones**: 'I Was A Boy' from *Take Your Experience and Peel It* (Indigo Dreams, 2016); **Philip Gross**: 'Sluice Angel' from *The Water Table* (Bloodaxe, 2009); **Patrick Lodge**: 'Panegyric for Cardiff Mods' from *Remarkable Occurrences* (Valley Press, 2019); **Sheenagh Pugh**: 'Toast' from *The Beautiful Lie* (Seren, 2002); **Paul Henry**: 'Arcades' from *The Brittle Sea: New and Selected Poems* (Seren, 2010); **Peter Finch**: 'St. David's Hall' and 'Words Beginning with 'A' from the Government's Welsh Assembly White Paper' are from *Selected Later Poems* (Seren, 2007); **Mike Jenkins**: 'Kairdiff Central Seagull' is from *Shedding Paper Skin* (Gwasg Carreg Gwalch, 2015); **Hanan Issa**: 'Grangetown' – new poem; **Abeer Ameer**: 'Roathed'. Commissioned by the Made-in-Roath festival, 2013; **Robert Walton**: 'Afon Rhymni' from *Sax Burglar Blues* (Seren, 2017); **Jonathan Edwards**: 'Half-Time Wales Vs. Germany, Cardiff Arms Park, 1991' from *My Famlly and Other Superheroes* (Seren, 2014); **Sarah Rowland Jones**: 'Spotted in the Hayes' – new poem; **Ifor Thomas**: 'I Loved Her A Lot In Splott' from *Unsafe Sex: New and Selected Poems* (Parthian, 1999); **Grahame Davies**: 'Capital Bookshop, Cardiff' from *Lightning Beneath the Sea* (Seren, 2012); **Dai George**: 'St. Fagan's, For The First And Last Time' from *The Claims Office* (Seren, 2013); **Tiffany Atkinson**: 'Daleks' from *Kink and Particle* (Seren, 2006); **Susie Wild**: 'The Bed Testers' from *Better Houses* (Parthian, 2017); **Stephen Payne**: 'The Girl on the Stairs' from *Pattern Beyond Chance* (HappenStance Press, 2015); **Kate North**: 'Cathays Cemetery' from *The Way Out* (Parthian, 2018); **clare e. potter**: 'Lunar Distance' – new poem; **Robert Minhinnick**: 'The Fox in the National Museum of Wales' from *New Selected Poems* (Carcanet, 2012).

Gillian Clarke

CITY

First, perhaps, we should view it across water,
passing two islands on a surging tide –
just short of the greatest rise and fall in the world.

Our ship would pitch where the sea wrestles the Severn,
muscular with rain from heart and hinterland,
sullen with slag and silky river silts.

Whoever they are, whatever tongue they speak,
from what continent, what distant island,
they crossed an ocean to help make the city.

Rounding the headland a hundred years ago,
most of them frozen, feverish, seasick, heartsick,
rolling up channel into the throat of the Severn,

they'd see the clock tower of the City Hall,
rumoured white buildings between broad avenues,
parkland and pleasure grounds beside the Taff.

For me it was 'let's pretend', lying awake
to the blink and sob of the Breaksea lightship,
my trip on the paddle steamer to Ilfracombe

a voyage from Africa, the *Cardiff Queen*
smashing the evening sea to smithereens,
a coming home made glamorous by dream

to a city we'd imagined into being.
Seeing's believing, believing's seeing.

Oliver Reynolds

TAFF

is a thief river
stealing from little hills
and sneaking to Cardiff
to paint the town black

has a dirty mouth
and colludes with the sea,
French-kissing the channel
all the way round to Brest

built a baulk for shipping
out of old prams, culm and mud
and gave it keel-snare names:
Cefn-Y-Wrach or *Hagback*

sidesteps the Arms Park
knowing that Terry Holmes'
bald patch started
when he fell in as a kid

didn't give a monkey's
when by its waters the psalmist
sat down yea, and wept:
the river just sniggered

tells the same story
over and differently over
and only ends its sentences
by beginning new ones

is a thief river

Gwyneth Lewis

'V' from *WELSH ESPIONAGE*

Welsh was the mother tongue, English was his.
He taught her the body by fetishist quiz,
father and daughter on the bottom stair:
'Dy benelin yw *elbow*, dy wallt di yw *hair*,

chin yw dy ên di, *head* yw dy ben.'
She promptly forgot, made him do it again.
Then he folded her *dwrn* and, calling it fist,
held it to show her knuckles and wrist.

'Let's keep it from Mam, as a special surprise.
Lips are *gwefusau*, *llygaid* are eyes.'
Each part he touched in their secret game
thrilled as she whispered its English name.

The mother was livid when she was told.
'We agreed, no English till four years old!'
She listened upstairs, her head in a whirl.
Was it such a bad thing to be Daddy's girl?

Damian Walford Davies

BESTIARY

I was there to cheer the follies
on the castle wall:

vulture, seal, beaver, imbecile
bear. Bravo the mad hyena! –

beefy snarler, hackles up,
scrabbling at the parapet

as the brass band played
The Man Who Broke the Bank

at Monte Carlo. A Lottie Collins
lookalike swanked on

to shriek *Ta-ra-ra boom-de-aye*
in a wicked Cockney drawl.

The beasts observed the party
from their heartless

height. I'd seen the lynx's
dead-pan stare before.

Mab Jones

I WAS A BOY

for Ernest Willows, the Cardiff airship pioneer

I was a boy, with a boy's
enthusiasm for flight –
things with wings and, later on,
balloons. At nineteen I exchanged
dentistry for dirigibles, the tombstone
rows of neat teeth for clouds.
Cumulus, Nimbostratus. Cirrus.
I repeated their names like a mantra
as I stitched the ribs of my first ship.
Finally, I rose, imagination's bubble
made rubber, gas, and metal.
Swami-like I swam through air, circling
the Eiffel Tower as a bumblebee
does a flower. Sometimes I dream
that I am sinking, my ship's skin alight,
and I am burning, trailing a tail
of flame as I fall. But then I wake and
I am boy again, with a boy's
idealism, innocence, and passion,
my airship still to be dreamt, then built;
imagination yet to spark, ignite.

Philip Gross

SLUICE ANGEL

Low tide at the sea lock,
     a forty foot drop to muddy shallows…
          One boat's width

     of channel that the dredger grubs up
          daily… Silt to one side scored in circles

          where they dragged for don't ask what…

The tall shut doors of the hall
     of the world at which the weight of water,
          of incipience, does not need to knock:

     feel it there like a shudder
          of difference, the engine of change.

          Now, almost soundless, hinges shift.

With a gradual calibrated rip
     like a concord of lathes, with a crypt smell,
          two green-grey-brown stiffening blades

     of water fold in. They curve, feathering
          themselves in free fall: wings

          flexed, shuddering, not to soar

but to pour themselves down, to earth
     the charge, liquid as solid as rock
          and untouchable, trouncing itself

     to a froth, to exhaustion, till with a sigh
          the gates can open, and the world,

          our world, small craft, come through.

Patrick Lodge

PANEGYRIC FOR CARDIFF MODS

White boys on the weekend searching for their soul;
sta-prest, back-combed, pilgrims at the Top Rank Suite.
It's the 60s man; see them dance, losing control.

Rondella, the Face, puppet master at the console,
loads the 45s, pulls the strings, that jerk loafered feet.
White boys on the weekend searching for their soul

to the liturgy of Stax, like postulants, shoal
close to the girls radiating risk, pubescent heat.
It's the 60s man; see them dance, losing control.

In the spots the dance floor is a goldfish bowl,
a land of a thousand dancers, steadfast in the beat.
White boys on the weekend searching for their soul,

an exodus from the suburbs, needing to become whole;
staunch as neophytes, they suck fierce on the music's teat.
It's the 60s man; see them dance, losing control

Fast forward fifty years, the faith remains whole;
a recalled underground life, transfigured and complete.
White boys on the weekend searching for their soul.
It's the 60s man; see them dance, losing control.

Sheenagh Pugh

TOAST

When I'm old I'll say *the summer*
they built the stadium. And I won't mean

the council. I'll be hugging the memory
of how, open to sun and the judgement

of passing eyes, young builders lay
golden and melting on hot pavements,

the toast of Cardiff. Each blessed lunchtime
Westgate Street, St. John's, the Hayes

were lined with fit bodies, forget
the jokes, these jeans were fuzz stretched tight

over unripe peaches. Sex objects,
and happily up for it. When women

sauntered by, whistling, they'd bask
in warm smiles, browning slowly, loving

the light. Sometimes they'd clock men
looking them over. It made no odds,

they never got mad; it was too heady
being young and fancied and in the sun.

They're gone now, all we have left of them
this vast concrete-and-glass mother-ship

that seems to have landed awkwardly
in our midst. And Westgate's dark

with November rain, but different, as if
the stones retain heat, secret impressions

of shoulder-blades, shallow cups,
as sand would do. The grey façade

of the empty auction house, three storeys
of boarded windows, doesn't look sad,

more like it's closed its eyes, breathing in
the smell of sweat, sunblock, confidence.

Paul Henry

ARCADES

Already you're gone, fixing your eyes
on a road's darkening arcade.

What song do you sing as the light fades?

The music shop you work in has closed
but I have to believe it is not too late.

Is it your eyes or your laugh I miss most?

I'd buy you those boots or that bracelet
your mother wore, or an amber ring

to prove it is not too late to sing,
to prove we are more than worn out ghosts.

Dream in arcades, love. Dream in arcades.

Peter Finch

ST. DAVID'S HALL

After the concert they come out: Dafydd ap Gwilym,
William W. Williams, Williamstown, Sion a Sian,
Ivor Emanuel, Lloyd George, Gelert, Owain Glyn Dŵr,
Mrs Davies Plas Newydd, Wyre Davies BBC
so glad there's no one here to mangle his name.
Some bear programmes like souvenir flags.
Their souls have been enlivened
by po-faced Elijah & enormous cymrectitude:
huge handbags, polyester shirts, those woollen celtic
drapes that make you look like an overweight bat, M&S ties.
They discuss school funding, where to go for supper,
death last week, look there's Alun Michael, disgrace,
that Ron didn't need Clapham we have our own parks,
chi wedi mwynhau, the timpani especially.

And there are the kids the ones who didn't bother to go in,
unworried about identity, sitting in the bar worse than Cerys,
Welsher than R.S., louder than Iwan Bala.
New Wales unselfishly immersed in the national pastime
alcohol alcohol antipathy antidote,
not mentioned anywhere in the Assembly agenda.
Dim pwynt see bachgen it's like breathing
you don't think, you do it, pwy yw Saunders anyway?
Over the speakers gloriously come the Furries

Mike Jenkins

KAIRDIFF CENTRAL SEAGULL

I've never felt threatened by a seagull before,
but this one's got 'STREET'
written along its beak,
which suddenly looks sharp
as a Stanley knife.

I wouldn't be surprised
by its swagger and attitude
if it wasn't into NWA or Tupac.

It eyes up my food
as if it already owns it
and I recall those stories of seabirds
snatching pasties or putting eyes out.

Those days spent by Aber pier
throwing crusts to balletic birds
seem a century away,
this creature's Kairdiff Central
born and bred, could pick
a packet from the rails
just before the inter-city's in.

It struts around me:
I am surrounded by a single bird!
Its pupils are two barrels
aiming straight at my cheese and celery.

I gulp the sandwich whole
like a heron with a fish.
Bro Seagull saunters off
to mug a kid with a burger.

Hanan Issa

GRANGETOWN

There's something about Grangetown.
Like an old blanket with mismatched squares,
it's stitched together from faraway places
all welcome, says the poster on the library door.
On Clare Road you can bump into a 'Salam'
then leap over dog-shit.
Men call to their mates across the street
as the no. 9 bus' husky breathing passes by.
Clouds of weed, greasy kebab smoke,
and the heavy dignity of bukhoor,
ripple in the air like the fluttering crisp packets under your feet.
Kids in white hijabs and hats, late for Quran school,
dodge an elder from the Hindu temple holding a bag of fruit.
Walk along the Taff and wave to the rowers
while looking for bodies in the watery murk.
Grange Gardens is either leafy quiet
or buzzing with delighted shrieks and scooters.
It's there I learnt about 'indecent exposure'
and how to walk on a tightrope.
At night, overhear the street menu
offered by cracked feminine voices
who just want business.
Oh, but the littering *ain't half bad round 'yer*.
Step carefully to avoid the spatter of lumps
that could be fat chips, could be vomit.
But at least Brutons is still here:
Fresh bread and a bag of welshcakes.
Say hello to the lady bent double with the shopping trolley,
who is shuffling to the hairdressers.
There's something about Grangetown.
It's the muck and the music: I love it.

Abeer Ameer

ROATHED

I've been 'Roathed'.
Utterly, stupendously, tremendously
eloped
with the Roath side of me
the cafes took me
to the East and deserted me
with the desserts
I've been veggied
in a yurt out back
strolled round the lake
sat on eulogy benches
swanned off with the swans
to be pooped on by the gulls.
I drank, ate,
read poetry at the Gate
was fleeced by a man
selling ice cream from a van
and stopped to smell the roses.
I took an oath this day
that come what may
I'll be
Monday, Tuesday, Wednesday,
Thursday, Friday, Saturday,
Sunday Roathed.

Robert Walton

AFON RHYMNI

There's no river like your first river
Down the years of your life, it rolls forever
At the end of Ball Lane you hear its call
From the hills to the sea, it flows and falls

There's no river like your first river
From the Beacons to the Channel, it rolls forever
At the end of Ball Lane it flows and falls
From Rhymney to the Lambies, you hear its call

There's no river like your first river
From Llanbradach to Llanrumney, it rolls forever
At the end of Ball Lane you hear its call
From Ystrad Mynach to Machen it flows and falls

There's no river like your first river
From Bedwas to Draethen it rolls forever
At the end of Ball Lane it flows and falls
From Bargoed to Rumney, you hear its call

There's no river like your first river
Down the years of your life, it rolls forever
At the end of Ball Lane you hear its call
From the hills to the sea, it flows and falls

Jonathan Edwards

HALF-TIME, WALES VS. GERMANY, CARDIFF ARMS PARK, 1991

Nil–nil. Once the changing room door's closed,
the Germans out of sight, the Welsh team can
collapse: there's Kevin Ratcliffe, belly up
on the treatment table; Sparky Hughes's body
sulks in the corner, floppy as the curls

which he had then. All half, they've barely had
a kick. Big Nev Southall throws his gloves
to the floor, like plates in a Greek restaurant
as, in tracksuit and belly, Terry Yorath
looks round at a room of Panini faces:

he doesn't know yet he will never get them
to a major finals. He does know what to say.
Ryan Giggs, still young enough to be
in a boy band, stands up, doing an impression
of his poster on my wall. The crowd begins

to ask for guidance from the great Jehovah
and Ian Rush's famous goal-scoring
moustache perks up. He's half an hour away
from the goal that cues the song that makes his name
five syllables. What he doesn't know

is I'm in the stand in my father's coat,
storing things to tell at school next day.
My father pours more tea from his work flask
and says *We got them now butt, watch* and asks
again if I'm too cold. What we don't know

is we'll speak of this twenty years from now –
one of us retired, one a teacher –
in a stadium they'll build down by the river.
But now it's Rushie Sparky Southall Giggs.
8.45: the crowd begins to roar,

wants to be fed until they want no more.
The tea tastes just like metal, is too hot
and something catches – right here – on the tongue.
The changing room door opens and they step out,
toe-touching, stretching, staring into the future –

it's time to be the people we'll become.

Sarah Rowland Jones

SPOTTED IN THE HAYES

on the last Wednesday in Advent
the new vicar, bobbing
through lunchtime crowds
in scarlet trench-coat
like a festive robin,
and tucked under her wing
a brand new ironing board –
one more means
to make the rough smooth
ready for the coming of the Lord.

Gillian Clarke

'WING' from *STADIUM*

Hare outrunning the pack.
Trick of the light.
He's not there, there,
a shouldering swerve,

foot, thigh, heart, eye,
sinew and nerve
too quick, too far
to see how, where,

with sleight of foot,
feint, flex and turn,
he dodges the charge
and breaks for the open

to a roar that enflames
the drums of his heart
and the single heart
of a multitude rising.

Ifor Thomas

I TOLD HER I LOVED
HER A LOT IN SPLOTT

I said I'd be sad if
she didn't come to Cardiff

I called her a sensation
when I met her at Central Station

I sang like a lark
when we walked in Roath Park

I said I'd never met anyone finer
in Rhiwbina

I vowed I'd be her man
in Penylan

I fell at her feet
in Oakfield Street

I told her I loved her a lot
in Splott

I said I liked having you
in Western Avenue.

But our love turned sour
over beer in the Glendower

She called me a fool
in the Empire Pool

She broke down and cried
in Riverside

After I'd let her down
in Grangetown

She shouted *YOU BRUTE*
in Bute

So we called it a day
In Manor Way

The next time, she said,
I'll get an A to Z

Grahame Davies

CAPITAL BOOKSHOP, CARDIFF

A battered volume that's seen better days
and on the flyleaf, in a careful hand:
"Dear John brought this the night he left Cathays."

It's Belloc's verse. Who reads him, nowadays?
Small wonder it's for sale, here, secondhand,
a battered volume that's seen better days.

There's more than love and leaving in that phrase;
a circumstance I don't quite understand:
"Dear John brought this the night he left Cathays."

The night he left. A parting of the ways
at evening time. Precipitate or planned?
A battered volume that's seen better days.

A goodbye stiff with silence and clichés?
And more than friendship when he took her hand?
"Dear John brought this the night he left Cathays."

A long-dead love; no record of it stays
except, on this old bookstall's bargain stand,
a battered volume that seen better days
"Dear John brought this the night he left Cathays."

Dai George

ST FAGAN'S, FOR THE
FIRST AND LAST TIME

The brutalist foyer a relic
from when everyone or, at any rate,
our architects had lost their minds;
water slugging lax through the mill
where the miller's on his one day off
in seven summers; a mother pig
writhing flat-out, dugs-up on the straw,
and you look as though you wish you were
already on the train, fleeing, when
if you can wait, there's a tram.

Honoured guest, I've one more stop
before we leave for home. Nobody
is ever impressed as we hope they'll be
and sure enough your hand in mine
wilts like a leaf on the tannery pool.
I catch myself wanting to thank you,
to make you understand: school trips,
nut brittle, the progress from cottage
to cottage – most of all that I want you
to stay and understand. But we make our way,

in silence, to Oakwood Workmen's Institute,
where we'll close, not with clipboards
and activities (*Year of establishment?*
Subsidies? Where onsite did I once skin
my knee?) but by peering over ropes
to where colliers read Dickens,
followed by my garbled lecture
on betterment – a principle I understand
as much as why tomorrow
I relinquish you to London.

Peter Finch

WORDS BEGINNING WITH 'A'
FROM THE GOVERNMENT'S WELSH
ASSEMBLY WHITE PAPER

a a assembly an assembly assembly assembly and assembly and assembly assembly assembly assembly assembly annexes and arrangements assembly and assembly affairs and authority accountability a achievement assembly autumn assembly a affect an an assembly assembly assembly and a alongside a an assembly assembly assembly allocate assembly and and acts assembly assembly assembly administrative agriculture a an annual and authorities and agency and authorities are accountable address assembly and answerable across assembly assembly assembly assembly assembly and arrangements are assembly assembly are assembly agriculture and and and and arts and annex a assembly approval assembly all after assembly assembly affairs and and assembly assembly and a and account appropriate assembly acts and are acta a assembly are assembly a authority and and able as and a assembly authorities agencies assembly able assembly assembly and a and ad a a a assembly assembly and able able assembly about a assembly and a assembly as appointments also assembly assembly an assembly assembly against as a able and authorities against and assembly are a and a assembly assembly and assembly assembly affairs assembly authorities and and and and all and ahead and are across and as assembly and assembly a attuned a agency and authority authority and and and and and any agenda assembly a assembly able a a a adopting assembly and and are a authority and afford an ambitious and a an as as an and air and agencies assembly a and administration agency a and assembly agency already an all and and and agencies authority authority as a and and assembling and authority are agency acquired and and address an a a across and assembly and appoint agency a a assembly authorities at and agency and a and an agency assembly assembly agency arrangements and agency authorities a and attracting and and assembly action action action and a and a assembly assembly agenda assembly at all agenda assembly and and appointments also and are also a and a and an authorities agencies and advice advice approximate a assembly and at affairs annual a and assembly and actions assembly assembly assembly and a administering assessment advisory assembly and adequate appropriate appropriate areas and approximate arrangements are appropriate approximate appropriate arrangements and assembly art assembly are arrangements approximate appricimate appropin approximarly approximin approximit approximate appropinate appropriate approlution approximate apprelin approling approve appross apprit approx. approximate appropriate assembly approt approt aprit aparse amprim aresenit aresenit arsenit areseit arsenit arsenit aresenit aresenit aresenit approximately assembly and arsen assembly all art and agriculture agenda appropriately alltittle all al aswoon apricot artle at assen ash arsenit assuitable assuage annual after amiddle approximate appealment apparliament arprat aprat art arse alltold approximate flatart anti anemia academic and averted arse art all assembly anti any attitudinal arseweakness all appropriate approximate approximate apripple affected arse affected all affected an any affected apathy apathy and responsibility for ancient monuments arses arses arses and wishing wells

Tiffany Atkinson

DALEKS

Back from the time-wars
like sixties kitchenettes *en pointes*,
and suicide bombers all. Scaling
Darwin's stairs a flight at a time
on human DNA, as if that should
be extraordinary these days. And

the Doctor's signed out of the series,
so it's showtime. Wartime. Bigtime.
The sets expand like space itself
to take the implications in. What
intergalactic temperospatial pyro-
technic brouhaha could take us

by surprise, unless our own pasts
twist beneath those clunky lids, with
one eye stalking out the future where,
and let's be frank, things turn out pretty
bleak? Come on. It's not for kids.

Susie Wild

THE BED TESTERS

Before breaking one,
we had hoped to make
this a career.

Post-coital thoughts acrobatic:
our entwined bodies bouncing
together, apart, in the hunt
for again, again,

again. Two years in and I am sprawled
across a mattress in IKEA
testing springs in electric
daylight, saying 'Remember

when…?' We look at foam
and latex, check for comfort against
budget, pretend to understand

the differences. We trolley our new buy
home, rolled up so impossibly small.
We wonder at how all
of that can be contained

within. We release it from
Its straps, wait for
the magic. It crackles, then bursts
to life with such delight.

We make love as if
It's our duty, fresh as that
first day, consider becoming
bed testers again.

Stephen Payne

GIRL ON THE STAIRS

The morning you had the test which revealed
the sex of our second child, sibling for Joel,
you chose not to phone but to drive unannounced
from the hospital to the campus, where you climbed
the stairs -- in your state! – to my sixth floor office
and ran into me somewhere around the fourth
rushing down to lecture with my head so full
of the General Problem Solver that when I unfolded
the scrap of paper pressed into my palm
as if it delivered secret instructions,
a password, or my role in a guessing game,
and read the single hand-written word *Girl*
I barely managed to return your smile
and to give you the quickest of kisses before
hurrying off, reluctant even to recollect
the encounter.   Eighteen years on,
the four of us together again for the weekend,
talking sexual politics at the kitchen table,
I can enjoy almost everything about it:
the stairwell with its echoes of unseen footsteps,
tall window edging you with a dazzle of white
Cardiff sky, the crinkled message in my fingers
and your breathless, uncrushable delight.

Kate North

CATHAYS CEMETERY

to Meryl

This long cut home is stuffed
with notable Anglicans,
Non-conformists,

   boxer, politician,
   soldier, bishop,

even Romans spread
flat across the bronze
winning view,

   collier, writer,
   magnate, surgeon,

loosened slabs silent
like an unlit match
the carriage porch

   cricketer, baron,
   aviator, victim,

memorials
creak at the push,
fresh beds sink,

   mixed heiress,
   plantation spinster
   helper of the blind,

a friend's husband,
a poem
their children.

clare e. potter

LUNAR DISTANCE

Whitchurch Hospital 1908-2016

Closing, this asylum, this place of healing,
this space of shouts and electrified erasing.   All things end. Except
time's passing and its holding still.
                                    Like your Smiths Amberley
Mantle clock,
                    the bent hour
                                    hand, the key you overwound,

gone now.
The corridor, bare – echoes wailing; yours from the jolt-room?

If we are vibrations, all, what air and light, what hand-touch of yours
meets mine, through an occultation of doors?

Did you thrash through this room (your arms tucked in that terrible jacket)?
Was this the cubical you were consigned to?

And had you noticed the same sharp corners
through the window, and that jackdaw –
                                    did you feed its mother's mother
with crumbs from your pocket
hoping it would send her up-valley to number 81,

                            so her wings

would beat time back
  to when your love was singing at the stove
            and you entered the house to it?

Robert Minhinnick

THE FOX IN THE NATIONAL MUSEUM OF WALES

He scans the frames but doesn't stop,
the fox who has come to the museum today,
his eye in the Renaissance
and his brush in the Baroque.

Between the dynasties his footprints
have still to fade, between the Shan and the Yung,
the porcelain atoms shivering at his touch,
ah, lighter than the emperor's breath, drinking rice wine from the bowl,
daintier than the eunuch pouring wine.

I came as quickly as I could
but already the fox had left the Industrial Revolution behind,
his eye has swept the age of atoms,
the Taj Mahal within the molecule.

The fox is in the fossils and folios, I cry.
The fox is in photography and the Folk Studies Department.
The fox is in the flux of the foyer,
the fox is in the flock,
the fox is in the flock.

Now the fox sniffs at the dodo
and at the door of Celtic orthography.
The grave-goods, the chariots, the gods of darkness,
he has made their acquaintance on previous occasions.

There, beneath the leatherbacked turtle he goes,
the turtle black as an oildrum,
under the skeleton of the whale he skedaddles,
the whalebone silver as bubblewrap.

Through the light of Provence moves the fox, through
the Ordovician era and the Sumerian summer,
greyblue the blush on him, this one who has seen so much,
blood on the bristles of his mouth,
and on his suit of iron filings the air fans like silk.

Through the Cubists and the Surrealists
this fox shimmies surreptitiously,
past the artist who has sawn himself in half
under the formaldehyde sky
goes this fox shiny as a silver
fax in his fox coat,
for at a foxtrot travels this fox
backwards and forwards in the museum.

Under the bells of *Brugmania*
that lull the Ecuardoran botanists to sleep,
over the grey moss of Iceland
further and further goes this fox,
passing the lambs at the foot of Jesus,
through the tear in Dante's cloak.

How long have I legged it
after his legerdemain, this fox
in the labyrinth, this fox that never hurries
yet passes an age in a footfall, this fox
from the forest of the portrait gallery
to Engineering's cornfield sigh?

I will tell you this.
He is something to follow,
this red fellow.
This fox I foster –
he is the future.

No one else
has seen him yet.
But they are closing
the iron doors.